German Shepherd

From Puppy to Adult (0–24 Months)

Written by:

Franklin Medina

www.simplyfordogs.com

Your Free Gift

As a way of saying thanks for your purchase, we're offering a free "A Dog's Best Diet" recipe book.

Visit Here to Access "A Dog's Best Diet" Recipe Book
https://Simplyfordogs.com/FreeEbook-German

Copyright © 2020 by Franklin Medina

All rights reserved. No part of this book may be used or reproduced by any means, graphic, electronic, or mechanical, including photocopying, recording, taping, or by any information storage retrieval system, without the written permission of the publisher except in the case of brief quotations embodied in critical articles and reviews.

Disclaimer

All rights reserved. No part of this book may be reproduced in any form without permission in writing from the author.. Reviewers may quote brief passages in reviews.

No part of this publication may be reproduced or transmitted in any form or by any means, mechanical or electronic, including photocopying or recording, or by any information storage and retrieval system, or transmitted by email without permission in writing from the publisher.

While all attempts have been made to verify the information provided in this publication, neither the author nor the publisher assumes any responsibility for errors, omissions, or contrary interpretations of the subject matter herein.

This book is for entertainment purposes only. The views expressed are those of the author alone, and should not be taken as expert instruction or commands. The reader is responsible for his or her own actions.

Adherence to all applicable laws and regulations, including international, federal, state and local laws governing professional licensing, business practices, advertising and all other aspects of doing business in the U.S, Canada or any other jurisdiction is the sole responsibility of the purchaser or reader.

Neither the author nor the publisher assumes any responsibility or liability whatsoever on the behalf of the purchaser or reader of these materials.

Any perceived slight of any individual or organization is purely unintentional.

CONTENTS

About the Author 1

About the German Shepherd 2

History 6

    A Change in Purpose 7

    Problems 8

    Hope for the Future 9

Appearance 10

    Coat 11

    Color 12

    Size 12

Temperament 13

    Reasons for Aggression 13

    Are German Shepherds More Likely Than Other Breeds to Have Temperament Issues? 15

    Beware of Public Perception 16

    Three Things – Socialize, Socialize, and Socialize 18

    How Is Temperament Created? 20

    Kids and Other Pets 22

    Finally… 24

Nutrition 25

Unique Requirements 26

Free Feeding 27

No Scraps! 28

Final Thoughts on Food 29

Grooming **30**

A Good Grooming Routine 31

Supplies 31

What If a Bath Is Necessary? 33

He's Gonna Shake! 34

He's Gonna Roll! 35

Shedding and Shaving 36

Eyes 37

Ears 38

Teeth 39

Paws 40

Finally… 42

Exercise and Toys **43**

Mixed-Age Households 44

Elderly German Shepherds 45

Toys 46

Squeakies 46

Plushies 47

Puzzle Toys 47

Balls 48

Finally… 48

Training **49**

House-Training 50

The Crate 50

House-Training Without a Crate 51

Don't Do This! 52

Be Patient 52

Obedience Training 53

Walking on Leash 53

Sit 55

Come 55

Down 56

Stay 57

Leave It 57

Don't Give Up 59

Health and Veterinary Care **60**

Hip Dysplasia 60

Elbow Dysplasia 61

Cataracts 61

Epilepsy 61

Gastric Dilation – Volvulus (Bloat) 62

Hemophilia 62

Diabetes 63

Panosteitis 63

Degenerative Disc Disease 64

Allergies 64

Pancreatitis 65

Bladder Stones 65

Nose Infections 65

Dental Issues 66

Cancer 66

Don't Panic 67

Finding the Right Veterinarian 68

Finally… 72

Bringing Your Dog Home 73

Day 1: Puppy-Proof 73

Day 2: Create a Calm Environment 74

Day 3: Identify a Sleeping Place 75

Day 4: Get Acquainted 75

Day 5: Expand the Space 76

Day 6: Build a Routine 76

Day 7: Start Training 76

Day 8: Visit the Vet 76

Day 9: Take a Look at Destructive Behaviors 77
　　Day 10: Kick Back and Relax! 77

Rescue **78**
　　Problems Specific to Rescue Dogs 83
　　Rescue or Not? 85

Housing **87**
　　Know the Rules 88
　　Consider Your Neighbors 89
　　Making It Work 89

Coming to the End **91**
　　When Should I Let My Dog Go? 91
　　A Dog's Prayer 92
　　So, When Is It Time? 93
　　Rainbow Bridge 93

Conclusion **96**

Sources **99**

About the Author

Franklin Medina is the founder and CEO of the hugely popular website SimplyforDogs.com. With his team of dedicated researchers, veterinary professionals, and content managers, Franklin brings his passion for "all things dog" to experienced dog owners and novices alike. In his spare time, Franklin enjoys coaching junior basketball and playing with his Shih-poo, Kobe.

About the German Shepherd

The German Shepherd Dog (GSD) is intelligent, capable, versatile, devoted, and courageous. These qualities, combined with a regal bearing and great work ethic, make the German Shepherd one of the most popular breeds in the United States. The breed is also very popular in Europe, where it is more commonly known as the Alsatian.

Originally bred for herding, the German Shepherd is a high-energy dog that requires a lot of exercise. If you're a couch potato, you should probably stop reading right now — the

German Shepherd is not the right breed for you. A Shepherd that doesn't get enough exercise is going to be irritable, frustrated, and destructive.

If you're considering a German Shepherd, you need to know that you're entering into a partnership. In exchange for food, affection, and sufficient mental and physical stimulation, your German Shepherd will return the love you give him tenfold and will be a loyal, valiant protector of you and your family.

German Shepherds have a stellar history of helping humans, from serving as guide dogs, to apprehending criminals, to providing security in airports and train stations, to serving as search-and-rescue dogs. Many German Shepherds were on-site in the rubble of the World Trade Center, finding survivors (and sadly, bodies), and also serving as therapy dogs for those who were traumatized by the events of 9/11.

For quite some time, the German Shepherd was considered the "gold standard" when it came to police work. Unfortunately, today's German Shepherd has fallen victim, as have so many other breeds, to extreme standards set for dog shows. Show standards have led to less powerful German Shepherds that aren't really up to the rigorous requirements of police work, and as a result, they have largely been replaced in police work by the more powerful Belgian Malinois. This does not mean, though, that a German Shepherd isn't well-suited to protect you and your family. There's still more than enough strength in the average Shepherd to make someone think twice before trying to do you harm.

If you've decided that the German Shepherd is the right breed for you, there should be little difficulty obtaining one. There are breeders all over the United States, and almost certain to be one in your area. Shepherds are also readily obtainable from animal shelters and rescue organizations, although I would caution you to ask a lot of questions about the dog's history if you decide to go this route. Sometimes, German Shepherds end up in shelters and rescue facilities because of temperament problems due to neglect or abuse, although it also happens when an elderly owner dies, or a dog has to be surrendered because of a change in the previous owner's marital or employment situation, or other factors that can make it impossible for a person to keep a perfectly good dog. I guess what I'm saying is simply this: make sure you know what you're getting into. A German Shepherd that's been rescued from a puppy mill or an abusive situation is not usually a good choice for a first-time owner.

If, after reading this brief overview, you think that a German Shepherd is the dog breed that speaks to your heart, continue reading. As you read this book, you will get to know the German

Shepherd. I'll take you through the history and characteristics of the breed, and we'll talk about temperament, training, exercise, nutrition, and more.

You will find, as you read, that some sections are long, and others are pretty short. That's simply because some topics need a lot of coverage, and others not so much.

If you're still wondering if a German Shepherd is right for you and your family, I believe that by the time you finish this book, you will be able to make an informed decision. If your heart is already leading you toward a German Shepherd, then by the time you finish reading, you'll have the tools you need to raise your German Shepherd from puppyhood through to the senior years.

It has been a great pleasure for me to write this book. I hope you enjoy reading it. Now, let's move on and talk in-depth about the remarkable German Shepherd.

History

The German Shepherd dates back just a little over 120 years, to 1899, and is, therefore, a relatively new breed. Not too many dog breeds can attribute their existence to a single person, and in this, the German Shepherd stands out, its existence being attributed to just one human: Captain Max von Stephanitz, a German cavalry captain who wanted to create the ultimate herding dog.

Long before von Stephanitz appeared on the canvas, farmers in Germany and the rest of Europe depended on large dogs to look after their herds. Often, shepherds would travel miles, over days at a time, to find a male dog worthy of their females. Until von Stephanitz, though, nobody came up with the idea of developing these herding dogs into a distinct breed.

When von Stephanitz retired from the military in 1898, he started experimenting with breeding. He looked at dogs throughout Europe, and he saw a lot of dogs that were outstanding when it came to intelligence, athletics, and capability. He did not, however, see a dog that had *all* of those traits. Then, one day, he went to a dog show, and noticed a dog that looked a lot like a wolf, and appeared to meet all his criteria. He bought the dog, and began breeding.

A Change in Purpose

Although he had intended for his breed to work as herding dogs, as Germany became more and more industrialized, von Stephanitz saw the need for such dogs fading. He was determined that his breed would continue as a working dog, and he decided that the dog's future was in police work and military service. He promoted his dogs to the German government, and during the First World War, his dogs served as sentries, guards, supply carriers, rescuers, messengers, and Red Cross dogs. Following the war, many American soldiers brought German Shepherd puppies home with them.

You've probably heard of one of those puppies. He was taken from a bombed-out kennel by an American soldier from Los Angeles, who trained him and then shopped him around to Hollywood. Rin-Tin-Tin went on to star in several movies, and at the height of his career, received more than ten thousand fan letters per week!

Problems

Von Stephanitz kept a close eye on what was happening with the breed and noticed that some issues were cropping up. By 1922, there was a propensity toward dental decay, and also some temperament problems. Accordingly, he instituted a system of quality control, insisting that before any German Shepherd was bred, the dog would have to pass tests based on health, intelligence, athleticism, and temperament.

Of course, this was taking place in Germany, and things weren't as regulated in the United States. Back then (as is the case now), the focus was on winning dog shows. The emphasis was on appearance — and we know that what looks good isn't necessarily what *is* good. Today's show standards have come very close to ruining what was once a noble breed.

Hope for the Future

Fortunately, some breeders reject the slender-hipped, low-slung standard that has become so popular. They are working to bring back the emphasis on strength and ability. Perhaps in the not-too-distant future, we will see a return to the German Shepherd von Stephanitz envisioned. In the meantime, there is still much to recommend the Shepherd. It would be going too far to say that the German Shepherd today is a shadow of what he used to be.

Despite the change in breed standards, the German Shepherd is still a good, strong dog, more than capable of serving as a friend and protector for your family. His intelligence, tenacity, and work ethic go a long way to offsetting anything that's been bred out in terms of strength. When it comes to love, loyalty, and pure devotion, a German Shepherd is an ideal choice for a canine companion.

Appearance

I could go on for pages and pages about the American Kennel Club (AKC) standard for the German Shepherd, but I'm not going to bore you with that. I'm assuming that you just want to know what a German Shepherd is supposed to look like, not how many centimeters long the ears should be. If you want the official standards, you can find them here, but for our purposes, I'm just going to talk about the general appearance of the German Shepherd.

The ideal German Shepherd should look agile and strong, longer than he is tall, with a deep body, and a muscular appearance. The head should be noble and proportional to the body. The eyes should be almond-shaped, and the ears should be pointed. A floppy ear is not all that uncommon in German Shepherds, but it will disqualify the dog from showing. The muzzle should be long and with a black nose. Any dog that does not have a black nose will be disqualified from showing.

Current show standards require a straight back, with high withers. The chest should be deep, and the ribs well-sprung. The tail should be bushy, and slightly curved when at rest — never curled forward. An overly curled tail is a serious flaw.

Coat

German Shepherds are double-coated, meaning that they have a thick, slightly wavy out coat, and a softer, downy inner coat. If the outer coat is too long, too curly, or too woolly, those are show flaws.

Color

German Shepherds come in a variety of colors, including black, black and red, black and tan, black and cream, black and silver, gray, blue, sable, liver, and white, most of which are acceptable at show. White Shepherds, however, are not permitted to show, and blue and liver are not desirable colors. Strong colors are preferred. If the coat is pale or looks washed out, that's a show flaw.

Keep in mind, when it comes to appearance, those coat colors have nothing to do with the health or ability of your dog. They're simply what's considered to be standard. If you're not interested in showing, coat color should not be a significant factor in choosing a dog.

Size

The average German Shepherd male should weigh between 66 and 88 pounds, and stand about 24–26 inches at the shoulder. A female should weigh 49–71 pounds, and stand 22–24 inches.

Temperament

German Shepherds are intelligent, self-assured, dignified dogs, with a high level of commitment to their humans. Sometimes, this commitment can manifest as aloofness toward strangers. However, once properly introduced, most German Shepherds will be cordial, if not overly affectionate, toward visitors. You can attribute this natural "standoffishness" to generation after generation of breeding for qualities desirable in a good guard dog.

Does this mean that German Shepherds are typically aggressive? No. It simply means that they have the *potential* for aggression and that this potential has to be properly channeled through close attention to training and socialization.

Reasons for Aggression

Every so often, you hear a dog owner say something like "I don't know what happened — he's always been the sweetest, gentlest dog in the world, and then yesterday, he tried to eat my neighbor! There was no reason; no reason at all!"

There is *always* a reason when a dog displays aggression. It's not that there isn't a reason; it's that you don't know what the reason is. It could be that the dog is frustrated because he's not getting the mental and physical exercise he needs. It might be that he has perceived a sudden move or a tone of voice that he thinks might constitute a threat to his family. In rare instances, aggression that *appears* to have no cause can be due to a head injury or brain tumor that went undiagnosed. In even rarer instances, aggression can be due to mental illness.

So, what's the takeaway here? It's this — know that there's always a reason for aggression. If you can identify it as being due to poor training, or poor socialization, then work with your German Shepherd to correct what's lacking. If you honestly can't identify the cause, then take your dog to the vet to rule out, or identify, an organic cause. If your dog is determined to be in good health, consider consulting an animal behaviorist and/or a professional trainer. Get the help you need before something bad happens.

Are German Shepherds More Likely Than Other Breeds to Have Temperament Issues?

From what I've just said, you might be wondering if I'm suggesting that the German Shepherd is a ticking time bomb, just waiting to go off. That's not what I'm saying — far from it.

The fact is that no breed gets a pass when it comes to temperament issues. Any dog can have temperament problems, and some breeds are simply more likely to be *perceived* as being of bad temperament. Usually, this perception is because of what people see and hear in the news, and neighborhood rumors.

Think of it this way — a Shih Tzu bites you. A Toy Poodle bites you. A Maltese bites you. What do you do in any of those situations? You disinfect the wound and slap on a Band-Aid. You make sure that the dog has had its shots, and you move on with your life.

Now, imagine that a 70-pound German Shepherd bites a person. This is a dog with a big mouth, big teeth, and big jaw pressure. If the injury is severe enough, and there are enough witnesses, the incident might end up on the news. At the very least, the neighborhood rumor mill is going to go into overdrive, and the owner becomes known as "that guy with the vicious dog."

Beware of Public Perception

Owners of any large breed will tell you that one of the biggest challenges they face is how other people view their dogs. Let me tell you a story.

When I was in my teens, I had a mixed-breed dog named Jake, and a best friend named Rita, whose family had two German Shepherds, Kelly and Kato. Every day after school, Rita and I would walk our dogs all over the neighborhood until the street lights came on, and we knew it was time to go home for supper. I couldn't begin to tell you how many neighbors who used to stop and pet Jake when he and I were out walking alone would cross the street when they'd see Kelly and Kato. And then came that fateful day…

Rita and her parents were going away for a few days on a ski holiday. Rita's father offered me the (then) princely sum of ten dollars if I'd feed, water, and exercise Kelly and Kato twice daily until they returned. He handed me the keys to the house, strapped the ski gear on top of the van, and then he, his wife, and Rita headed off for the mountains.

That afternoon, I went down for the first go-round with Kelly and Kato. As soon as I unlocked the door, they bounced out of the house and, being so happy to see me, knocked me down — I wasn't a big kid, and they were big dogs! I laughed, snuggled them, snapped on their leashes, and set off.

Fast-forward one hour. I got back to the house, and there was an animal control van sitting in the driveway, and a stern-looking man waiting, holding a four-foot restraining pole.

Remember, I was just a kid, so I was like, "Ummm…. Hi…."

"We had a report of a dog attack," he said.

Half an hour later, we had it all straightened out, but that didn't stop the neighborhood rumor mill — I'd been attacked, there was blood all over the driveway, I was in the ICU and not expected to live, the dogs were going to be put down… and all because of a perception of bad temperament in German Shepherds.

What I'm driving at here is that when you own a certain breed of dog, like a Rottweiler, a Doberman, a Cane Corso, and yes, a German Shepherd, you are going to have to be very vigilant when it comes to making sure that everyone who meets your dog forms a positive impression of his temperament. An individual German Shepherd is no more likely than an individual dog of any other breed to have temperament issues, and any dog, given the right provocation, can bite. If a dog bites and is of a breed that is *perceived,* rightly or wrongly, to have temperament issues, the cry to have the dog destroyed will be loud and long.

Make sure that your German Shepherd is *known* to be of good temperament. That way, if at some point your dog is provoked to the point of biting, you can recruit friends and neighbors who will say, "He's a good dog. Whatever happened, it couldn't have been his fault."

How do you achieve that? Three things.

Three Things – Socialize, Socialize, and Socialize

Some breeds seem to be practically *born* socialized. Labrador Retrievers and Golden Retrievers top the list for this kind of temperament, and yet they're among the breeds most likely to have bite statistics recorded against them.

Does this have anything to do with the inherent nature of the breed? No. What it has to do with is the prevalence of the breed. Labs and Goldens are among the most popular breeds in the United States, and therefore, the breeds with the most bite counts recorded against them. More Labs, more Goldens, more bites.

It's the same with German Shepherds. The German Shepherd is a very popular breed, occupying the number-two spot among 196 AKC-recognized breeds. This means that there will, inevitably, be bites recorded against the breed.

How can you be sure that your German Shepherd will be friendly and welcoming?

The answer is that you can *never* be 100 percent sure, not with any breed of dog, but there are things you can do. As soon as you bring your German Shepherd puppy home, start taking him places. Take him to doggie daycare, where he can meet other humans and other dogs. Take him with you when you go shopping, and hang out in the parking lot — you can bet that any number of people are going to come over to your car and ask if they can pet your cute puppy. Call your kids' school and ask if you can bring your puppy over at recess to play with the children. Invite neighbors in. Take your puppy on walks around the neighborhood, where he can experience all kinds of different situations.

An ounce of prevention is worth a pound of cure, as my mother used to say. So socialize, socialize, socialize!

How Is Temperament Created?

Temperament is created in two ways: with the influence of genetics, and with the influence of the environment. Accordingly, if you're looking to buy a German Shepherd puppy, you have to look at the parents, and look at how the puppy has been raised.

The very first step is to visit the breeding kennel. The owner of the kennel should be more than happy to have you visit the mother of your puppy and the rest of the litter. You might not be able to see the father, since not all kennels keep breeding pairs. Not being able to see the father isn't a red flag — he might be off-site. But if you can't see the mother, something is wrong.

The kennel should be clean, and the breeding bitch should be friendly. If she's fearful or aggressive, something is wrong. If the breeder doesn't want you to see the kennel and suggests bringing the puppy and the bitch to another location for you to meet, something is *very* wrong. Chances are you're dealing with a puppy mill. One huge tip-off in cases like this is the bitch's feet — if they're soft, she's probably been caged. Her feet have never touched the ground, because she's been caged, usually in deplorable conditions. Just don't put yourself in the position of having to check — always visit the kennel.

Now, remember again that not all puppies are created equally. Even in the best litter, you might find a puppy that has issues. Don't choose the puppy that is cowering in a corner, away from his littermates — you might feel sorry for him and feel as though you need to rescue him, but you could be setting yourself up for temperament issues later on. Instead, choose the "middle of the road" guy — the one who isn't cowering, but also isn't bullying his littermates — he's just kind of hanging out and getting along with everyone.

If you perceive a temperament issue in a German Shepherd puppy that you're thinking of buying, ask yourself if you might be dealing with a puppy mill. If you think you are, run, don't walk, to another breeder.

Kids and Other Pets

The German Shepherd can be a very good fit for households where there are children and other pets. As a general rule, though, when dealing with cats and other small animals, it's best to introduce a German Shepherd puppy to an adult animal. This is the case with virtually any breed of dog.

German Shepherds are typically very good with kids within their family. That said, they might not be quite as good with visiting children. As I've already stated, German Shepherds are very protective of their humans, and your German Shepherd might perceive a difference between *his* kids and *visiting* kids. What might look, to you, like normal play among children could be perceived by your German Shepherd as aggression. When your kids' friends come to visit, supervise closely.

For that matter, supervise your kids when they're playing with the dog. Teach your kids that ear pulling, tail pulling, and other rough handling is *not okay.* Until they're old enough (usually around age 12) to know how to treat a dog respectfully, assume that bad things could happen, and keep a close eye on kid/dog interactions.

Finally…

To sum it up, German Shepherds don't typically have serious temperament issues. They're smart, protective, and, although a bit aloof, are not likely to be aggressive toward visitors to your home. They're good with kids but must be supervised, especially with visiting children. Because of their size, though, they could accidentally hurt toddlers. If you're bringing a German Shepherd into a home with small children, it's up to you, as the responsible adult in the equation, to make sure that there's an atmosphere of mutual respect.

Nutrition

Much of the time, dog owners overthink food. I've raised any number of dogs on nothing more than generic food, with the approval of my veterinarian. That said, I have to admit that not all generic foods might contain what your German Shepherd needs. You have to consider a lot of things — your dog's height, weight, energy level, and environment.

Depending on where your German Shepherd is in terms of growth, from puppyhood and beyond, his nutritional requirements could vary significantly. Just as an example,

German Shepherds (like other large breeds) tend to need a lot more protein than other dogs — as much as one-quarter of their entire diet! So you have to consider age, weight, height, and more. Your German Shepherd might need more food, less food, vitamin supplements... well, you get the idea. If you're in doubt as to what constitutes the best diet for your German Shepherd, consult your veterinarian.

Unique Requirements

As a general rule, German Shepherds have much the same dietary requirements (in terms of nutrient content) as other breeds of similar size. Most German Shepherds are very energetic, though, and may need slightly higher quantities of food. A German Shepherd that is older and less energetic may need lower quantities to prevent undesirable weight gain.

It's not rocket science. If your German Shepherd is packing on too many pounds, reduce the amount of food. If he seems to be a bit too thin, give him more. German Shepherds are large dogs, usually weighing between 60 and 90 pounds. The average adult German Shepherd needs about 2,000 calories per day to maintain his optimum weight and energy level.

It's important to feed high-quality, age-appropriate dog food, and to keep in mind that your German Shepherd will have different dietary needs at the various stages of his life. Like most dogs, German Shepherds love their food, so it's important not to overfeed.

For the purposes of this book, I am assuming that you have purchased, or will be purchasing, your German Shepherd. You are not breeding, so you don't need me to tell you that a German Shepherd puppy should nurse for at least eight weeks, along with taking solid food as soon as he can chew. Once you have your puppy home, you should feed him a quality puppy chow four times a day at regular intervals for the first 12 weeks of age. Take away any uneaten food after 20 minutes.

Once your puppy reaches the age of three months, you can decrease the feedings to three times a day. By six months, offer the puppy chow twice daily. At a year, you can begin feeding adult food twice a day.

Free Feeding

As an alternative to scheduled feeding, you might want to consider free feeding. With this method, you simply fill a container with dog food and let your dog eat whenever he pleases. This is not a good method to use with wet dog food, but I hope you're not feeding wet food in any case — dry food is much better for your dog.

If your dog household is multi-generational (some of your canines are on puppy chow and others on adult food), you will not be able to free feed. If you can free feed, though, it can be very convenient. If your schedule is erratic and you're not able to commit to a feeding routine, free feeding can be the best way to ensure that your German Shepherd gets all the nutrition he needs, whether you're there or not.

Free feeding has another advantage. If a dog is free-fed from the beginning, he will not view food as an "event" and will be unlikely to eat more than he needs. Free-fed dogs seldom develop weight problems. When they do, it's usually because the human in the relationship, who can't resist those big brown eyes, has been offering too many treats.

No Scraps!

If you're of a certain age, you probably remember a time when what your dog got to eat was whatever was left over after your family had their meal. That wasn't the best idea, as the food could have contained bones, spices, little in the way of what a dog needs in the way of nutrition, and maybe even some things that are very bad for dogs.

Your dog is not a human, and should not be fed in the same way that humans are fed. Did you know, for instance, that a single handful of grapes can cause your dog's kidneys to fail? Tomatoes are equally hard on the kidneys, so think twice before you give your best buddy that leftover pizza or spaghetti.

Anything containing xylitol, which is an artificial sweetener, can deliver a death sentence.

Final Thoughts on Food

German Shepherds don't require a whole lot in terms of special feeding. Almost any good-quality dog food will suffice. You can feed on a schedule, or free feed — whatever works best for you. As long as your German Shepherd gets a proper balance of protein, fats, carbohydrates, and other essential nutrients, he'll maintain a healthy weight and keep his energy level up.

As to what not to feed your dog, click here for a brief overview. Remember, too, that Google is your friend, and you can find any number of sites that will go into great detail on what is and isn't appropriate for your dog when it comes to human food treats. Always read labels carefully — most people don't know, for example, that although peanut butter is generally a very healthy treat for dogs, some brands contain the deadly xylitol.

If you're still obsessing over what constitutes the best diet for your German Shepherd, you have another friend: your veterinarian. If your German Shepherd has specific dietary requirements due to age, obesity, allergies, or any other conditions, your vet can recommend the best food.

Grooming

You might think that a German Shepherd, being such an active dog, would be a nightmare when it comes to grooming. That actually couldn't be further from the truth. The hair is long and has an undercoat, but doesn't tend to mat, and regular brushing will take care of most dirt. The natural oils in the coat also make brushing very easy.

Once in a while, a bath might be needed, but Shepherds are usually pretty cooperative when it comes to soap and water. It doesn't hurt, though, to introduce baths at the puppy stage, whether they're needed or not. It's just a way of getting your German Shepherd used to baths before he reaches a size where manhandling him into a bathtub is going to be problematic.

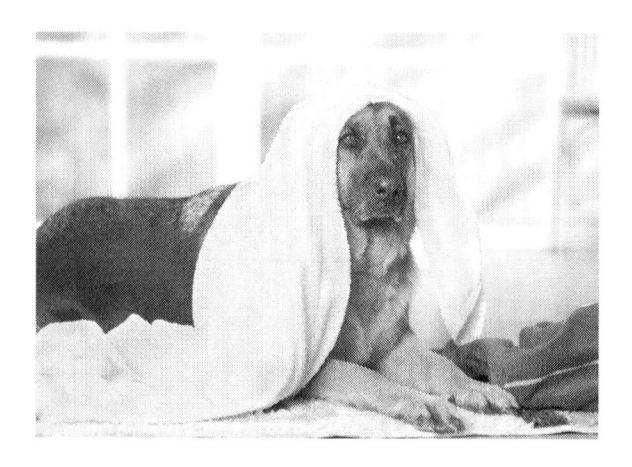

That said, there's more to grooming than just brushing and bathing.

A Good Grooming Routine

Your German Shepherd will love being brushed whether he needs it or not. It makes for great bonding time, and while you're brushing, you can use the opportunity to take a look at his ears, eyes, teeth, paws, and body, to make sure that everything is as it should be.

Check for scrapes, cuts, ticks, fleas, and any other problems. Make sure he doesn't have any broken nails. Look inside his mouth and ears to make sure everything looks pink and healthy. Look at his eyes to make sure they're not red or watery. If you perceive any issues, take him to the vet to be checked out.

Most German Shepherds are not resistant to this type of checkup, especially if you start when he's a puppy. If he seems a little anxious, give him lots of praise and treats — he'll come around in no time.

Supplies

German Shepherds don't require a lot in the way of grooming supplies. They're not prone to skin problems, so most of the time, almost any dog shampoo will get the job done. A couple of good brushes and you're generally good to go. In the material that follows, though, you'll learn about a few different supplies that you can use, or not.

1. Clippers

    You might want to buy a set of clippers if your Shepherd isn't in the habit of walking on hard surfaces that will naturally wear down his nails, or if you're not planning on taking him to a professional groomer to have his nails done.

    There are two basic types of clippers: the guillotine, which has a blade that slides shut and closes, and the scissor-type, which is… well, like a pair of scissors! Either type is effective. You can also use a Dremel tool to grind the nails down, although some dogs dislike the sound of this type of tool.

2. Tooth Care

    Dogs can develop dental issues in the same way as humans can, so if you can get your dog to tolerate tooth brushing, it would be a very good idea. Get a toothbrush that's made specifically for dogs, and use a specially formulated toothpaste. Human toothpaste is not good for dogs — it often contains ingredients that can be harmful. Your pet supply store can offer you a wide range of flavored toothpaste specifically made for dogs.

3. Rubber Curry Comb

   This is one of the best grooming tools for your German Shepherd. It's similar to a curry comb that is used for horses. It fits in your palm and has rubber teeth that loosen your Shepherd's undercoat, bringing dirt and dead hair to the surface.

4. Slicker Brush

   This is a rectangular brush with thin bristles made of wire. It gets rid of dirt, loose hair, and knots.

5. Bristle Brush

   This is a brush that you'll use for finishing up the grooming. It's lightweight and works to distribute the natural oils throughout the coat. It's very gentle, so well-suited to use on delicate areas like the tummy and the insides of the legs.

What If a Bath Is Necessary?

As previously suggested, unless your German Shepherd gets into something exceptionally filthy, you will not likely need to bathe him. If you do have to, though, you want to make sure that the procedure is as pleasant as possible. Accordingly, there are a few things you should do.

First, your German Shepherd is not likely to appreciate the shampoo, no matter how gentle it is. Put a couple of drops of mineral oil in his eyes before you begin to protect him from irritation, and make sure to use a tearless shampoo specially formulated for dogs.

It also wouldn't hurt to insert a cotton ball into each ear to keep water from getting in. Sometimes, water in the ears during a bath can lead to infection. Of course, you'll want to remember to take the cotton balls out after the bath.

Using warm water — not hot — soak your dog's hair completely. Make sure that you get through the thick undercoat, all the way to the skin. A hand-held shower attachment can be your best friend.

Now, lather up and massage the shampoo all through your Shepherd's coat. Rinse thoroughly until the water runs clear. Make sure to get all the shampoo out — if you don't, your dog's skin is going to be irritated.

He's Gonna Shake!

This is an absolute given. There is no way that your freshly bathed German Shepherd is not going to shake after a bath, no matter how quickly you wrap him in a towel. Just let him do it, and then go to work with the towel.

He's Gonna Roll!

This is another given. Any dog, of any breed, after a bath, is going to want to roll. Preferably in something stinky. If you can bathe your German Shepherd inside, do so. If you must bathe in the yard, then keep in mind that what is "stinky" to you might smell very good to your dog.

The good news is that what smells good to you also smells good to your dog. He doesn't necessarily have to roll in poo. What he wants is a really strong smell so that he can say to himself, "Okay, here I am!"

You know how little foo-foo dogs get perfumed at the groomer? It's not because they're sissies.

Well, maybe they are, but that's a whole other topic for discussion, in another book. Those little dogs get perfumed because they like strong scents, and perfume is just as good as poo when it comes to keeping them from rolling.

A perfume will work just as well on your big, strong German Shepherd. To keep him from rolling, apply your favorite perfume or aftershave. Your dog just wants to smell *something,* and as long as the scent is strong, it will prevent him from rolling in things that you would prefer *not* to smell.

Shedding and Shaving

As to shaving, no. Just NO.

You may have heard from well-meaning idiots that it's a good idea to shave your German Shepherd in the summer to keep him from being too hot. This is a bad idea. Your German Shepherd's coat protects him from all kinds of weather, and shaving takes away that protection. In the winter, it makes him cold. In the summer, it makes him vulnerable to sunburn. And despite what you might have heard, it will not stop shedding.

Most German Shepherds will shed heavily twice a year, and quite a bit year-round. You can deal with this by brushing or petting, but never by shaving. If the shedding seems excessive, see your veterinarian. He could have an allergy or another condition that is causing him to "blow hair."

Eyes

To inspect your German Shepherd's eyes, pull his ears back gently. Since his ears are pointed, you shouldn't have to pull too much, but this will open his eyes, which should be clear and bright. There should be no redness in the eyes. Take a look under his eyelids, using your finger to inspect the lower lid. Then pull gently upward to check out the upper lid. You should be seeing pink tissue. If it looks red, he might have irritation due to dirt under the eyelids, and a vet visit is warranted.

Most dogs, German Shepherds included, will develop what most people call "eye boogers." This is just a whitish discharge that can be easily wiped away with your fingers or a damp cloth. If the discharge is yellowish or greenish, though, it would be a good idea to take your buddy to the vet to rule out infection and get medication if necessary.

If your dog's eyes ever look bluish or cloudy, a vet visit is *absolutely* warranted. This could indicate cataracts, and if not treated, your dog could go blind.

Ears

It's easy to check a German Shepherd's ears, since they're open and pointed. Just take a look inside to make sure that there are no damp, dark areas where fungus can grow. After bathing or swimming, you should always dry your German Shepherd's ears thoroughly to prevent this from happening.

It's also a good idea to clean your German Shepherd's ears weekly. This is easy to do. You do it the same way you'd clean your ears. Don't use Q-tips, since it's easy to push them in too far and injure the eardrum. Use cotton balls or pads with a bit of dog-friendly cleaning solution, and massage the solution into the ear to loosen wax and dirt.

If your dog wants to shake his head, let him. This will loosen any dirt. Keep wiping using clean cotton balls or pads, working near the ear canal and then wiping away in order to take the dirt out of the ear. Repeat as needed. Then wipe with a clean, dry cloth.

Teeth

Again, thinking back to how dogs were cared for back in the day, most people wouldn't have thought that brushing their dog's teeth was something that was needed. We know better now.

Dogs can be prone to dental decay in the same way as humans. If your dog's teeth aren't cleaned, he can end up with the same dental issues that humans have — cavities, abscesses, the need for root canal, and so on. Tartar and plaque can build up and cause infections and gum disease.

You can prevent dental disease in your German Shepherd with proper diet and oral care. Brushing is best, but not all dogs will tolerate it. If your dog hates having his teeth brushed, you can prevent the buildup of plaque and tartar by feeding a dog food that is specifically formulated to keep the teeth clean. You can also offer things like carrots, broccoli, and other hard vegetables that work to remove plaque and tartar from the teeth. Hard toys can also help with dental issues.

The best way of preventing dental decay, though, is through brushing. Most dogs aren't crazy about having their teeth brushed, so go about it slowly. Start when your German Shepherd is just a puppy, using just your finger to massage his gums. As he gets used to it, you can introduce a brush and dog toothpaste. Remember that dental infections can cause a lot of trouble later on — not just in the gums and teeth, but in the heart and other organs. It's vital that you catch dental infections in the beginning, and have them treated.

Paws

If your German Shepherd is outdoors a lot, you'll want to check his feet regularly. Check for abrasions, cuts, embedded stones, and splinters. If it looks like anything is embedded, you can use tweezers to take it out, provided that whatever is there isn't too deep. Then you can apply an antiseptic to the affected area. If your dog is limping, it's vet time.

Insect stings can also cause limping. If you suspect a sting, then apply a cold compress to the affected area, and watch for swelling or respiration problems that could be an indication of an allergic reaction. Any difficulty breathing is cause for an immediate vet trip.

No limp should ever go untreated. Even if you don't see a cut, sting, or abrasion, you should take your dog to the vet if he's limping. It could be an indication of a sprain or even a broken bone.

Another thing that can cause your dog to limp is chemicals that are applied to snowfall. If you live in an area where salt or other substances are applied to snow on the roads, they could be hurting your dog's paws. Chemical burns can be nasty.

As to the nails, keep them short. If they get long, they can affect your dog's gait. Overly long nails can also damage your floors. Worst-case scenario, if you have carpet, your dog's nails can get caught in the pile and end up being ripped off. That's very painful for the dog.

When trimming your dog's nails, watch for the quick. It's a vein that runs down the middle of the nail, and if you clip it, it can bleed. Your dog will be hurt. If you do mess up and cut the quick, use a cotton swab or a Kleenex to put pressure on the nail until it stops bleeding. Then use styptic powder and keep the dog calm until the bleeding stops.

When trimming, don't forget the dewclaws. These are the claws that grow up the back of the front legs, and if they're not trimmed, they can grow into the leg.

Finally...

Grooming should be easy and pleasant. Whatever you're doing with your dog, praise him often, and give him treats. If you're worried about grooming at home, take your dog to a pro. There's no shame in it. Any discomfort with grooming on your part could distress your dog, so let someone else handle it.

Exercise and Toys

German Shepherds are high-energy dogs that love physically demanding tasks. Originally bred for work, a German Shepherd is well suited to run and hike for hours, even under difficult conditions. This means that even though the German Shepherd's role today is primarily to be a family pet, nothing has changed in terms of genetics — the German Shepherd is still bred to want and need a significant amount of activity.

German Shepherds that don't have an opportunity to dissipate their pent-up energy can become anxious and destructive. If you're something of a couch potato, the German Shepherd may not be the right dog for you. People who are not prepared to give a German Shepherd the exercise it needs often end up with barking, digging, chewing dynamos, and it's their fault. Lack of sufficient exercise can also lead to obesity, which can result in damaged joints, high blood pressure, and an increased risk of heart disease and diabetes.

So, how much exercise does your German Shepherd need? Generally speaking, an adult German Shepherd will require about two hours of walking or other exercises daily. For German Shepherd puppies, use the "five-minute rule," providing five minutes of exercise for each month of your puppy's age. For the first few months, you don't have to worry about a structured exercise regime in the form of regular walks. Most German Shepherd puppies will wear themselves out just during the course of play.

Mixed-Age Households

If you're introducing a puppy into a household that is already occupied by an elderly dog (and many owners do this, "staggering" their dogs so that they are not without a canine companion once the older dog passes), you will need to supervise play to ensure that the younger dog does not overwhelm the older one. You don't want an older dog to become overexerted. By the same token, a German Shepherd in the prime of his life can easily exhaust a puppy, and that could lead to the puppy's developing joints sustaining damage. When there's an age discrepancy, keep an eye on your dogs and make sure that they get enough rest.

Elderly German Shepherds

Eventually, your German Shepherd is going to slow down. For most German Shepherds, this happens around age 7, although some remain very active well into the double digits.

As your German Shepherd ages, keep an eye out for signs of hip dysplasia, arthritis, and other issues that could keep him from enjoying the same amount of exercise that he did in his younger years. For an elderly German Shepherd, swimming is great exercise, since the water supports and eases the pressure on the limbs. If swimming isn't an option in your area, gentle walking is best. If you're in doubt as to how much exercise your older German Shepherd should get, consult your veterinarian.

One of the most important things to keep in mind when considering exercise for an elderly German Shepherd is that he may try to do things he's not really up for, in order to please you. He thinks, "Mom loves throwing the ball for me, so I'll keep chasing it even though I'm tired and sore. Dad loves long hikes, and I love Dad, so I'm going to do my level best to keep up with him."

You have to be the responsible party in this human–canine relationship. Don't put your dog in this position.

Toys

German Shepherds, being highly active dogs, need a variety of toys for both indoors and outdoors. You'll need toys that help your dog to blow off energy, as well as toys that challenge the mind.

Generally speaking, toys for German Shepherds need to be very durable. You have a powerful dog with a strong bite, so cheap dollar-store toys aren't going to last more than a few minutes. They can also present a choking hazard once your German Shepherd has finished making short work of them. You're far better off to invest in a few quality toys from a reputable pet supply store.

Squeakies

Most German Shepherds love squeaky toys. You may have heard that squeakies activate the prey drive and encourage aggression. I disagree. All dogs have some level of prey drive, and it is high in German Shepherds. So should you use squeaky toys?

I view squeakies as a harmless way of channeling the prey drive into play. So if your German Shepherd loves squeakies, get him some! Make sure, though, that they're well-made. The last thing you want is for your dog to rip the toy apart and swallow the squeaker.

Plushies

Some dogs love nothing more than wandering about the house, carrying their favorite plush toy. Others see plushies as things to tear apart and leave strewn to all corners of the home.

I wouldn't advise buying your German Shepherd a whole lot of plush toys at once. If you have a "shredder," you're just going to end up wasting a whole lot of money. Try him with one, and see how it goes. Make sure to buy a quality toy, though — again, avoid the dollar stores. Cheap toys are easily destroyed, and may even contain harmful materials.

Puzzle Toys

Puzzle toys provide mental stimulation for your dog. You hide treats inside the toy, and your German Shepherd has to solve the puzzle to get the treats. These toys can provide hours of enjoyment when you're not available to play with your dog. A bored dog is a destructive dog, so if you have to leave your dog alone while you're at work, shopping, or whatever, make sure he has puzzle toys to keep him entertained.

Balls

What dog doesn't love balls? When choosing a ball for your German Shepherd, remember that he has a fairly large mouth. The ball should extend a bit over the sides of his lips — too small, and it could present a choking hazard.

If you find that your arm is getting tired from the constant throwing while playing fetch, you might consider investing in a ball thrower. This is a device that holds the ball and allows you to launch it without straining your arm. You can play for as long as your Shepherd wants, without straining your muscles.

Finally...

Exercise is essential for your German Shepherd. Give him as much as he needs, and watch to make sure he's not getting *more* than he needs. Toys can help you with exercise, as well as providing your dog with a source of amusement when you're not available.

Training

Every dog needs basic house-training and obedience training, and German Shepherds are no exception. You house-train, obviously, because unless you're a total pig, you don't want dog waste in your home. As to obedience training, it helps your dog to be a good canine citizen, and can even save his life in a variety of situations.

You should begin house-training as soon as you get your German Shepherd puppy home. As for obedience training, you can give him a few days to get accustomed to his new surroundings, and then begin teaching him simple commands.

House-Training

Unless you plan on having your German Shepherd outdoors all the time (and I seriously hope you don't, because leaving your dog alone in the yard is just about the nastiest, cruelest thing you can do to an animal who wants nothing more than to be with you), you are going to have to house-train your German Shepherd puppy. Left to his own devices, a puppy will eliminate wherever it's convenient. He has to be shown where it's okay to "go," and where it's not okay.

The Crate

When house-training your German Shepherd puppy, a crate can be very helpful. You may have heard people decry the use of crates, saying things like "I want the whole *house* to be his crate! It's not fair to lock him up!"

In a way, those people are right, but they're also wrong. Yes, it would be horribly wrong to keep a dog constantly confined to a crate. On the other hand, most dogs have no objections to occupying a crate from time to time — it's their own place, where they feel safe. It's also a place where they're not going to want to do their business, since dogs generally dislike eliminating where they sleep.

To crate-train, feed and water your dog in the crate. You can put toys and treats in the crate to make him feel more comfortable. About half an hour after he's eaten, take him outside and wait for him to pee and poop. At night, make sure he's had an outdoor potty trip, and then let him sleep in his crate. If he has to go out during the night, he will probably alert you with whining or barking rather than mess where he sleeps.

House-Training Without a Crate

If you're not using a crate, you will have to be super-vigilant when it comes to your German Shepherd puppy's eliminatory needs. Watch him after feeding and watering for any signs that he needs to go out. Ideally, be proactive — take him out *before* he needs to go, and then wait until he's done his thing.

Don't praise your puppy for peeing and pooping in the yard. All he's going to learn from that is that you praised him for peeing and pooping — not that you praised him for doing it in the right place. Just let it be business as usual, and then bring him inside.

Never punish your German Shepherd puppy for doing his business in the house. Accidents are going to happen — that's what they make soap and water for! If you scold him or punish him, all he's going to learn is that, next time, it would be better for him to do his thing in a place where you're less likely to find it. Just keep on with the regular trips outdoors, and soon he'll get the idea that the yard is where you want him to pee and poop.

Don't Do This!

I can't believe that there are still people who think that a good way to house-train a puppy is to rub his nose in his urine or excrement. Dogs have no objections to strong smells, and your puppy will have no idea why you're doing this. It's not going to stop in-house urination and defecation, and it's just flat-out a stupid thing to do. So don't do it.

You might also hear from people who think that a whack on the snout with a rolled-up newspaper is a good way to discourage messing in the house. It's not. It's abusive. Don't do it.

Be Patient

House-training a German Shepherd puppy isn't all that difficult. It takes patience, and you're going to have to accept that there will be a few accidents. Most puppies catch on quickly, though, and house-training shouldn't take more than a few weeks.

Obedience Training

All dogs need basic obedience training. It works in two ways — first, if you obedience-train your dog, he will be easy to handle. That's no small thing when you're dealing with a dog that can weigh upwards of 70 pounds. Second, it works to keep your dog safe — if he knows that he needs to do what you tell him, you won't have to worry about him wandering into traffic or other dangers.

Walking on Leash

The first thing your German Shepherd puppy should learn is how to walk on a leash. Most places have leash laws, and besides, keeping your dog on a leash ensures his safety.

It's not hard to train a German Shepherd to walk on a leash, but it's something that is best done early. A puppy will learn quickly that a gentle tug on the leash means he should move toward your side, and a puppy is easily managed — a full-grown Shepherd, not so much!

To teach your German Shepherd puppy to walk on a leash, place him opposite your dominant side. Pull gently on the leash while saying "heel." When he's close to you, with his head approximately opposite your knee, tell him what a wonderful dog he is, and give him a treat. Rinse and repeat. He'll get the idea in no time.

Sit

Once your dog is used to the leash, it's time to teach him to sit. This is a very easy command for your dog to learn, and it's the foundation for the other commands you will teach your dog.

With your dog on a leash, hold a treat just above his nose. Raise your hand. Your dog's head will naturally follow the direction of the treat, and at the same time, his bottom will lower. Once he's sitting, give him the treat and lots of praise. Repeat until he'll sit without needing the treat.

Come

This is a very important command, as it's the one you'll use to get your dog back to where you are if he gets away from you. Face it, stuff happens — you might accidentally leave the gate open, or lose your grip on his leash, and the last thing you want is for him to run into danger.

Put your dog on-leash, and then lean down so you're close to his level. Say "Come," and pull gently on the leash. When he reaches you, give him a treat and lots of praise. Once he'll come consistently when on a leash, take the leash off (this is best done indoors) and continue to practice the command. Again, treats and praise will go a long way.

Down

We're moving now into the more difficult commands. Most dogs don't like being placed in a "down" position, because it's submissive. Don't attempt it if your dog is feeling anxious — wait until he's more relaxed, and then give it a go.

You'll need a high-value treat for this exercise. Place one in your hand and close your fist. Then, hold your hand next to your dog's nose. As he sniffs it, lower your hand to the floor and slide it toward you, encouraging your dog to follow your hand from a lowered position. Once he's down, say "Down," praise him, and give him the treat.

You may need to repeat this several times. If your dog tries to get up or lunges at your hand, tell him "No." Take your hand away. Don't try to force him into position. Just go back to the beginning and keep trying until he gets it right.

Stay

This is another command that can be a bit hard to teach. Your dog wants to be next to you, and telling him that he has to be farther away can be problematic. Before you work with "Stay," you should have "Sit" nailed down.

Place your dog in the sit. With your hand up, palm outward, say "Stay." Take a step or two back, and if your dog stays, tell him what a wonderful, amazing creature he is, and give him a treat. Always offer a reward, even if he only holds the stay position for a few seconds.

Gradually increase the number of steps you take back and the length of time you expect your dog to hold the stay position. If your dog can't maintain the stay for any length of time, don't get discouraged — this is a difficult command to master for most dogs. It takes time and patience.

Leave It

Dogs being dogs, they often get into things that can be nasty, or even harmful. Is there a dog that doesn't love garbage, or won't grab a chicken bone if one is within reach? I haven't met one.

That said, I have a friend who breeds Rottweilers, and one day while I was visiting, I observed her gigantic (140 pounds, probably) male grab a chicken leg that she'd accidentally knocked on the floor while preparing our lunch. Without missing a beat, my friend reached halfway down the dog's throat, said, "Give me that," and extracted the chicken leg (we didn't eat it!).

"How," I asked, "is it that you can just reach in and take something like that?"

She pondered for a minute, and then said, "I guess it's just because it never occurred to me that I couldn't." Upon further pondering, she told me that she'd always taken things away from her dogs, from puppyhood onward. She'd begin by giving them their meals, taking them away, giving them back, taking them away… and so on. Her dogs got used to having things only when given, and to giving them up when she asked.

Start early with this one. Puppies have sharp little teeth that can give you a nasty graze or even draw a bit of blood. An adult Shepherd that doesn't want you to have something can cause significantly more damage.

Put a treat in each hand, and close your fists. Hold out one fist toward your dog, and say "Leave it." He's allowed to sniff, paw, mouth, and even bark a lung up trying to get you to give him the treat, but he isn't allowed to take it. Once he stops trying to get the treat in the hand you've held forward, give him the treat that's in the other hand.

If you do this often enough, your dog will eventually begin to move away from the first hand. It's his way of telling you, "Okay, I get it, I can't have this treat but maybe I can have the other one."

At this point, your dog should be making eye contact with you when you say "Leave it," and you're ready to move on to the next step. Take a high-value treat in one hand, and a low-value treat in the other. Put the low-value treat on the floor, covering it with your hand. Say "Leave it." Wait until he looks at the floor, and then give him the better treat and lots of praise.

Don't rush this. Giving up any kind of treat is a lot to ask of your dog. If he doesn't nail it right away, just keep on trying. Eventually, he'll get it right.

Don't Give Up

Some aspects of training are going to be easy. Others are going to take a bit of work. Always use positive reinforcement — treats and praise — never punishment. Remember that your dog wants to please you, so give him the encouragement he needs to do just that. With love and patience, you'll be able to teach your German Shepherd all the things he needs to learn to be the companion you will love for as long as he lives.

Health and Veterinary Care

German Shepherds are not known to have a lot of health problems, but there is no such thing as a perfectly healthy dog breed. Some conditions can affect German Shepherds. It's unlikely that your German Shepherd will ever become unhealthy, but in the interest of full disclosure, I'm going to tell you about some of the conditions that could affect your dog.

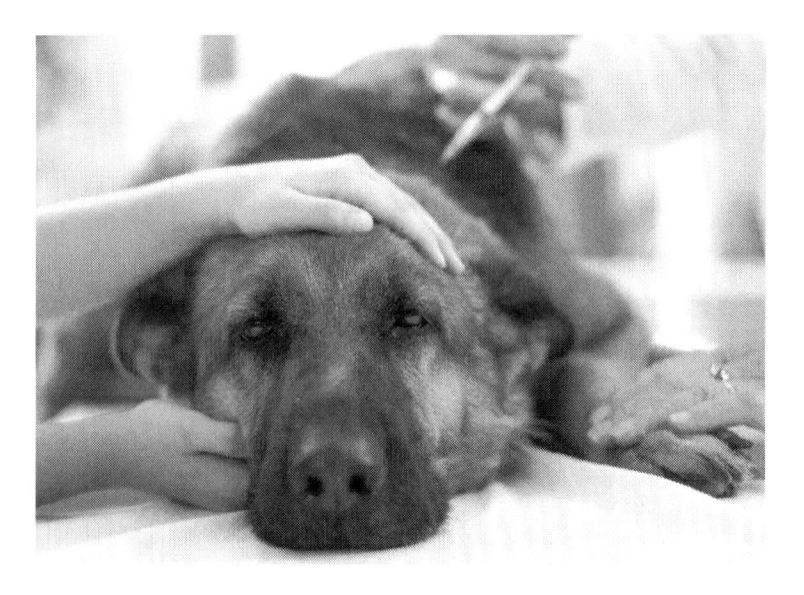

Hip Dysplasia

This is an inherited condition in which the thigh bone and the hip joint don't fit together as they should. Some dogs will show no symptoms at all, while others may display lameness in one or both of the hind legs. As the dog grows older, the condition can lead to arthritis. Dogs with hip dysplasia should not be bred.

Elbow Dysplasia

This condition occurs when the three bones making up the elbow grow at different rates. It can cause lameness. Most of the time, elbow dysplasia can be treated with medication. In extreme cases, surgery may be required. As is the case with hip dysplasia, German Shepherds that have been identified as having elbow dysplasia should not be bred.

Cataracts

As is the case with humans, cataracts in dogs manifest as cloudy spots over the lens of the eye. They're most common in elderly dogs but can occur at any age. They may, or may not, impair vision. Cataracts can be hereditary, so dogs that develop the condition should not be bred.

Epilepsy

German Shepherds sometimes suffer from epilepsy. Seizures can be mild (usually identified as unusual behavior, like staggering or running frantically) or severe (in which the dog spasms uncontrollably). Usually, the condition can be controlled with medication. It is important, though, to note that seizures can be due to other causes — head injuries, for example. If your Shepherd is having seizures, see your vet immediately.

Gastric Dilation – Volvulus (Bloat)

This condition is more common among giant breeds like Mastiffs and Great Danes, but isn't unheard of in other deep-chested breeds like German Shepherds. Bloat occurs when the stomach takes in too much gas or air, and then twists. The dog can't vomit or belch, and the blood flow to the heart is reduced. The blood pressure is lowered, the dog goes into shock, and if left untreated, the dog will die.

If your dog seems depressed, weak, displays a rapid heart rate, is retching without vomiting, is drooling excessively, or has a distended abdomen, suspect bloat and contact your veterinarian immediately.

Hemophilia

German Shepherds that come from long interbreeding lines may be prone to hemophilia, which is a condition in which the blood does not clot properly. German Shepherds with hemophilia will need to be closely monitored during surgery, even with routine operations. There is no cure for hemophilia, but under close supervision for bumps, bruises, cuts, and so on, a German Shepherd with hemophilia can live a long, happy life. As is the case with all hereditary ailments, though, if your German Shepherd has been diagnosed with hemophilia, do not breed.

Diabetes

German Shepherds are sometimes born with diabetes, and at other times develop it later in life due to overeating and lack of exercise. It can usually be controlled with diet and proper exercise, and in more severe cases, with regular insulin injections.

Panosteitis

This is a condition that's usually diagnosed fairly early on — before the dog reaches two years of age, and sometimes even before six months. It's often called "growing pains," because large breeds frequently experience discomfort as their bones and joints grow. It's not harmful, and it's not permanent. However, if a dog doesn't "grow out" of it, then it could be something else. If what appears to be panosteitis lasts longer than two years, see your veterinarian.

Degenerative Disc Disease

Many large dogs can have spinal problems, and German Shepherds are no exception. Spinal conditions can be difficult to diagnose, and sometimes perfectly responsible breeders can inadvertently sell puppies that are prone to degenerative disc disease. When good breeders know that their animals are prone to this condition, they won't breed, but sometimes mistakes happen.

There is nothing that can be done to prevent degenerative disc disease, but there are measures that can be taken to prevent it from getting any worse. Proper diet, exercise, and good nutrition can go a long way toward helping a German Shepherd with degenerative disc disease to live a long, healthy life.

Allergies

Nobody knows why, but German Shepherds seem to be a lot more prone to developing allergies than other dogs. Most often, a German Shepherd is allergic to corn, gluten, and rice. The condition is easily treated simply by avoiding foods that contain these ingredients.

Pancreatitis

This condition is an inflammation of the pancreas. Usually, it's caused by eating too much fat, so if your idea of giving your dog a treat means trimming the fat off those pork chops you're cooking for your dinner, just stop doing it! Your dog is not a garbage disposal!

Bladder Stones

If you notice that your German Shepherd is straining when he urinates, chances are he's developed bladder stones. These are calcified deposits in the urinary tract that can block the normal flow of urine. At best, they cause discomfort. At worst, they can completely block the urinary flow, cause urine to build up in your dog's kidneys, and can be fatal.

Any straining while urinating should be taken very seriously. If your German Shepherd is constantly wanting to go outside, but never producing much in the way of urine, get him to the vet immediately.

Nose Infections

Many dog breeds are prone to nose infections, and I wouldn't say that German Shepherds are any more vulnerable than other breeds. This is just something to keep in mind regardless of what breed of dog you have. Sinus passages can often become inflamed, resulting in discharge from the nose, coughing, or sneezing. There might also be a discharge that contains pus.

A nose infection isn't likely to kill your dog, and it's not a "get to the vet *this minute*" situation. It will make your dog very uncomfortable, though, so book a vet appointment to get the treatment your dog needs to recover quickly.

Dental Issues

German Shepherds seem to be more likely than other breeds to suffer from dental infections and tooth decay. Proper oral hygiene is a must. While some breeds are fine with tooth brushing once a week, you should go the extra mile with your German Shepherd and brush several times a week, or even daily, if possible.

Cancer

This is the word that strikes terror into the heart of owners of certain breeds — Rottweilers, Boxers, Golden Retrievers, and, sadly, German Shepherds. Knowing that your dog is among the breeds most likely to die of cancer is, quite simply, the price you pay for loving that breed.

Common cancers in German Shepherds include lymphoma (a cancer of the lymphatic system), melanoma (skin cancer), and osteosarcoma (bone cancer).

Now, before you decide that you can't possibly have a German Shepherd because of the prevalence of cancer in the breed, consider this. The average life expectancy for a German Shepherd is 9–12 years. Cancer in German Shepherds does not usually occur *before* 9 years. That means that you *already* got the expected lifespan out of your dog. Anything else is a bonus.

It's pretty much a given that most of us are going to outlive our dogs. Don't let what is going to be a probable cause of death stop you from having a German Shepherd, if that's the breed that speaks to your heart.

While your German Shepherd is unlikely to suffer from all or even a few of these issues, when considering purchasing a puppy or adult dog, it is important to know what kind of health problems to look out for and what kinds of health problems you might have to face in the future.

Don't Panic

Most German Shepherds will never develop any of these conditions. Forewarned, though, is forearmed.

Finding the Right Veterinarian

Finding the right veterinarian for your dog is every bit as important as finding a general practitioner for yourself. You'll want to consider several factors — your dog's breed, his age, any medical conditions he might have, and so on. Here are some things to consider when choosing your dog's veterinarian.

1. Proximity

    This might not seem like a huge deal to begin with, but if you have an emergency and you need to get to the veterinarian right away, the last thing you want to have to do is drive for miles. If you can find an animal hospital that is close to your home, that's something to consider. On the other hand, though, if you feel that your dog would get better care at a clinic a bit farther afield, consider that as well.

2. Recommendations

    I can probably sum this up in one sentence — if everybody and their dog (sorry about that) tells you, "Don't go to Dr. X," then don't go to Dr. X. There is almost certainly a reason. Most veterinarians are wonderful and caring, but in the same way that there is a preponderance of arsonists in fire departments, dentists who enjoy their patients' pain, and doctors like Harold Shipman, there are a few bad vets out there.

    Talk to fellow pet owners, family, and friends. Find out who they like and would recommend. You can also talk to local breeders who have the skinny on veterinarians in your neighborhood. Veterinary societies can also help you to determine where to take your dog.

3. Go Visiting

    One of the most important things you can do when choosing a veterinarian is to visit the animal hospital before you commit. On the first visit, go without your dog, and just take a look around. Find out what the hours are, and what services are provided. Make sure the clinic is clean and the staff seem to be knowledgeable and content in their job. Ask about the average wait time for appointments, and find out if you can request a specific veterinarian, or if it's luck of the draw.

If everything looks good, pay another visit, this time with your dog. How does the staff react to your buddy? Are they happy to see your German Shepherd, showering him with love and treats, and making him feel like the most special dog in the world? Or are they rushed and eager to get on to something else?

4. Ask About Specialty Services

If your dog needs dental care, radiology, chemotherapy, or other specialty services, are they available on-site, or will you need to wait for a specialist to visit the clinic? If specialists are not available for regular visits, does the animal hospital have an arrangement with another provider to guarantee that your dog will get the care he needs?

5. Ask About Fees

Generally speaking, fees at veterinary clinics should be just about the same from one clinic to another. If the fees seem unusually high, they're gouging. If they're unusually low, they're cutting corners somewhere. Select a "middle of the road" clinic. Then, ask about what methods of payment are accepted. Will the vet provide a written estimate for services rendered? Will you be informed at every step of treatment what the cost is going to be? If you have pet insurance, does the clinic accept your particular plan? If you can't pay all at once for services, will the clinic allow you to set up a payment plan?

I know that when it comes to a dog's health, most people are just going to say, "Fix my best friend; I don't care what it costs." That said, though, a good animal hospital will work with you in such a way that paying for your dog's care won't break you in the short term.

6. Look into Accreditations and Experience

    You've probably seen ads for various companies, touting "Over 50 years combined experience!" That's just lovely, except that sometimes it means that the company has something like a hundred staff members, each of whom has six months' experience. That doesn't do much good, does it?

    So, how many vets and vet techs are on staff? And how much *individual* experience do they have? Do the people identified as technicians have any real education and experience, or are they just glorified receptionists? Is the clinic accredited by the AAHA (American Animal Hospital Association)?

7. But Don't Put Too Much Stock in It

Having said all that, keep in mind that sometimes accreditations mean nothing more nor less than a piece of paper that can be put in a frame and displayed on the clinic wall. Here's what really matters — is your German Shepherd treated like an honored guest when he visits the clinic? Do you feel that your concerns are heard? Do you feel as though the clinic staff is going to treat your Shepherd as if he were their own? Do you feel comfortable? If the answer to any of these questions is "No," then find another animal hospital.

Finally...

Ensuring your dog's long-term health is what has to be done to have him enjoy a good, long life. This means understanding the conditions that your dog could be prone to, and making sure that you find the right veterinarian. Don't obsess over illnesses that your German Shepherd may never develop, but make sure that you have the right veterinary clinic in case they do.

Bringing Your Dog Home

You might wonder why I've left this section toward the latter part of this book. It's because I didn't want to waste your time. If you read a few chapters and decided that a German Shepherd wasn't right for you, you wouldn't have wanted to slog through a chapter about bringing home a dog that didn't fit your lifestyle or family. If you've read this far, though, I think you've made your decision. So let's take it day by day for the next 10 days — here's how you bring home your new best friend!

Day 1: Puppy-Proof

Before you bring your new buddy home, you're going to have to do pretty much the same things you would do if you were getting your house ready for a toddler. In other words, you have to take a look around and make sure that there's nothing that could be dangerous.

Are household chemicals out of the way? Are there any electrical cords within reach? Are there gaps in the fence? Are there children's toys that could present a choking hazard?

Check out your house thoroughly, and make sure that there's nothing that could present a danger to your German Shepherd puppy.

Day 2: Create a Calm Environment

Your German Shepherd puppy is going to be confused and probably a bit scared. Don't introduce too many people all at once. Rather than opening up the entire house, keep your puppy in just a couple of rooms. As time goes by, you can introduce other family members and open up other rooms.

Day 3: Identify a Sleeping Place

Decide where your German Shepherd puppy is going to sleep. It can be in a crate, a basket, or at the foot of your bed. Whatever works for you. Keep it consistent, though, and don't be upset if your puppy whines and whimpers through the night to begin with. He's not used to this new space, and it will take time for him to get used to it. Make sure he gets regular bathroom breaks, especially before bedtime.

Day 4: Get Acquainted

By this time, your German Shepherd puppy should be accustomed to his new surroundings, although it would still be best to keep the explorable space to just a few rooms.

This is the point where you're going to get to know each other better. If you can, take some time off work so that you can spend several days with your new puppy. Take time to just be with him, and take him for walks around the neighborhood. This is the time when you'll cement the bond the two of you will have over the rest of your lives.

Day 5: Expand the Space

Open up a few more rooms, and let your German Shepherd puppy explore the house. You'll still have to watch him closely, but let him get used to his new surroundings.

Day 6: Build a Routine

Set a schedule for walks, training, rests, games, and more. Dogs tend to be creatures of habit, and they appreciate knowing what's going to happen, and when it's going to happen.

Day 7: Start Training

You really can't begin training too early. Good training makes for a good dog, so start with the basics like walking on a leash, sit, stay, and so on.

Day 8: Visit the Vet

You're going to want to have your German Shepherd puppy vet-checked, and this is a good time to do it. He feels safe with you by now and is ready to meet other people.

Day 9: Take a Look at Destructive Behaviors

All puppies are destructive — it's just the way they are. They'll bite your ankles, chew your belongings, and generally run roughshod over your household.

This doesn't mean that your puppy is bad — it just means that he's a puppy!

You will want to deal with those behaviors, though, so make sure to offer lots of toys and treats to offset undesirable behavior.

Day 10: Kick Back and Relax!

You've come a long way, and so has your German Shepherd puppy! Congratulate yourself on everything you've achieved. Snuggle with your new friend. And tell yourself, "I did a good job!" Because you did!

Rescue

If you are the type of person who wants to help a dog that's having a rough go of it, then all I have to say about you is that you're a wonderful human being, and I admire you. Any German Shepherd would be very lucky to have you as his mom or dad.

Before you commit, though, let's talk about some of the reasons why dogs end up in rescue facilities, and how you might deal with the issues that led up to it. Here they are, in no particular order.

1. Things changed.

    As of the time of this writing (November 2020), we're viewing everything through the lens of Covid-19. All over the world, people are dealing with changes wrought by this pandemic. For many people, one of the most devastating changes has been the loss of employment.

    Picture yourself in this scenario: Because of the pandemic, you have been laid off, furloughed, downsized... Whatever term you choose to use, the upshot is the same. You're out of work. When you first got your dog, you could afford food, training, veterinary care, grooming, and so on. Now you're barely making ends meet, and you have to make the difficult decision to surrender your dog. He could live for many more years, and you want them to be good years. You want him to have access to the things you can no longer provide. So, your heart is broken, and your dog is now awaiting rescue.

There can, of course, be other situations where a change in circumstances can lead someone to surrender a dog. In a scenario like this, there's no downside to rescuing. You'll be helping out a good person and a good dog.

2. The owner died.

    Whether it's due to illness, old age, or an accident, the sad fact is that sometimes people do not outlive their dogs. If no family member or friend is willing or able to take the dog, then the dog could end up in a rescue facility.

If the dog is surrendered because the owner died of old age, then there is one thing you'll have to think about — old people usually have old dogs. This is simply because, at some point in a person's life, even if that person has always had a dog, they begin to think about the possibility of outliving the dog. People in their 60s and 70s often say to themselves, "This had better be the last dog."

When you rescue a senior dog, you'll have to accept that your time with him will be limited. There will also be the veterinary costs associated with giving an elderly dog a good quality of life. I'm not saying that you shouldn't do it — just that you should go into it with realistic expectations.

3. The dog has behavioral or aggression issues.

    German Shepherd dogs can be aggressive if they've been abused, so if you're not an experienced dog owner, I wouldn't recommend a German Shepherd rescue. If the issue is neglect, though, you can take a German Shepherd into your home and your heart without worrying about aggression.

    Sometimes, dogs are surrendered due to poor training. Unfortunately, there are people out there who are incapable of training their dog or are simply disinclined to do so. Then, through no fault of his own, a dog that isn't house-trained, lunges on lead, is destructive, runs into traffic, or engages in other undesirable behaviors ends up looking for a new home.

    Behavioral issues can be corrected, usually quickly, with training. Aggression issues may take some time to work out, but love and patience can work wonders.

4. A puppy mill got busted.

    If you're looking to rescue a German Shepherd puppy, it's highly unlikely that you'll find one that's ended up in a facility due to the death of the owner, loss of income, or behavioral issues. It's far more likely that that sweet little soul who has captured your heart has come from a puppy mill that's been shut down.

A puppy mill dog, of any breed, is not a rescue that should be undertaken by an amateur. If you choose to rescue a puppy, you can be assured that he will not have had enough time with his mother and the rest of the litter — most puppy-mill animals are sold far too young. It takes at least eight weeks for a puppy to be weaned and to have learned what he needs to learn, from Mom and siblings, about being a dog. Puppy-mill operators don't care about this, and will often sell puppies as early as four weeks.

Puppy-mill puppies also don't get the veterinary care they require. You can probably forget about initial shots and worming.

If you take an adult dog from a puppy mill, you will almost certainly be in for a world of grief. Breeding dogs and bitches are kept in horrific conditions and deprived of the socialization they need to be good dogs. The best-case scenario here is that you will be dealing with a dog that is afraid. The worst-case scenario is that the dog will be so unhealthy and so frightened that he will never be normal in any reasonable sense of the word.

If you are imagining long, leisurely walks, games of fetch and Frisbee, and snuggles on the couch once the day is done, you may never get this with a puppy-mill rescue dog. Your rescue dog may not even want to be touched. All you can do in a situation like that is defer to your rescue dog — he's not used to being handled in a kind fashion, if he's been handled at all. Essentially, you're adopting a dog that has special needs, and if you're not up to that, please don't rescue a puppy-mill dog.

Problems Specific to Rescue Dogs

Rescue dogs, unless it's a situation like I described earlier where a dog ends up in a shelter because an elderly owner has died, often come with problems that need to be corrected.

1. Urinating in the house
   Often, dogs end up in rescue shelters simply because they're not house-trained. This is one of the easiest problems to overcome. Just look at the previous material on house-training, and whether you're dealing with a

puppy or an adult dog, proceed accordingly. Don't get angry, don't scold, and don't punish.

2. Chewing

   Much of the time, a rescue dog will chew, especially if he's been taken from a puppy mill. It's simply because he's never had toys, and he sees whatever is there as something to play with. Offer a firm "No," take him away from what he's chewing, and give him a toy.

3. Barking

   Dogs bark for any number of reasons — they're not getting enough attention, they're bored, they're lonely, and yes, sometimes dogs bark because there *is* a threat out there!

   Don't discourage barking. Find out why your dog is barking, and then react accordingly. If it's boredom or loneliness, play with him! If he's alerting you to a threat, tell him he's a good boy, and then give him a treat when he quiets down.

4. Pulling on the leash

   This is easy. Tell your dog to heel, and give him a treat when he stops pulling. Rinse and repeat.

5. Jumping

   Sometimes, rescue dogs get so excited they just can't help jumping on you. If your dog jumps, just ignore him. Turn your back on him and let him bounce off. There is no reward, and there is no punishment. It's just that nothing happens, so there's no need for any kind of reaction. If he's not rewarded in some way for the behavior, the dog will stop the behavior.

6. Aggression

An abused German Shepherd could be aggressive, as could any dog of any breed. Minor aggression doesn't necessarily mean you should throw in the towel, as it can often be corrected with firm training. On the other hand, if you're afraid of your German Shepherd rescue, you might want to get some professional help. Pro trainers know how to deal with growling, snapping, and snarling. The main thing is not to let the aggressive behavior continue. The longer it goes on, the harder it is to correct. There's nothing wrong with saying, "I want to help this dog, but I'm out of my league."

Rescue or Not?

If you're new to the German Shepherd or to any other breed of dog, I wouldn't recommend that you consider a rescue. You might get a perfectly lovely dog from a perfectly lovely home. On the other hand, you could end up with a dog that has serious issues that you'll be ill-equipped to deal with. Instead, find a good breeder with good dogs, and start from that point. Once you know more about the breed, and dogs in general, you can consider rescuing if that's something that appeals to you.

Remember that rescuing a dog is a huge commitment. Much of the time, you're taking a damaged animal that needs a lot of training, and a lot of love. If you're not up to it, don't do it.

Housing

I've emphasized over and over that German Shepherds are active dogs. But what if you live in a tiny house or an apartment, and your heart tells you that you just *have* to have a Shepherd? Can you?

Yes, you can. The best fit for a German Shepherd is a house with a good-sized, fenced-in yard. However, a Shepherd can live comfortably in an apartment or a small house. You will, however, have to make sure that your Shepherd gets all the exercise he needs. This means at least a one-hour walk every day. You will, in other words, have to make up for the lack of space with a lot of time spent outside. If you live in a high-rise, it would be best to make sure that there's a dog park nearby.

A Shepherd is a big dog — usually upwards of 70 pounds. A studio apartment probably isn't going to be the best accommodation, but a decent-sized apartment is okay for a German Shepherd that gets regular exercise.

Know the Rules

One thing you have to keep in mind is that some landlords will restrict the size of dog you can have. You might end up being charged an enhanced damage deposit, or even monthly fees if you have a dog of a certain size.

Is that fair? No.

Is it legal? Yes. The sad fact is that your landlord can impose any regulations he or she likes when it comes to the size of your dog. All I can say here is that before you commit to accommodations, make sure you know what your landlord has in mind when it comes to the breed of dog you have chosen.

Consider Your Neighbors

If you have a German Shepherd puppy, remember that this can present its own challenges. For one thing, puppies tend to bark, howl, and whine until they learn when it is and isn't acceptable. Your neighbors might not like this. As your puppy becomes socialized, then barking will lessen. It might not hurt to visit your neighbors and apologize in advance for any noise — this will earn you brownie points, and besides, it takes an awfully hard heart to be angry with a puppy!

Making It Work

Here are some suggestions that can ease the difficulties of living in a rental unit with a German Shepherd.

1. If possible, choose an apartment on a lower floor. In your German Shepherd's first year, it's best to curtail (as much as possible) trips up and down stairs. This prevents strain on your dog's developing joints.
2. Start potty training early, and make sure to thoroughly clean up any accidents. If you have to move, you want to be assured of getting back your damage deposit.

3. If your Shepherd has separation anxiety, consider a dog-sitter or doggie daycare for the times when you have to be away. This will go a long way toward preventing destructive behavior.
4. If you can, take a few days off work to help your German Shepherd become accustomed to his new surroundings.

German Shepherds are wonderfully adaptable and can live almost anywhere. They only need two things — enough exercise, and *you.*

Coming to the End

When I write these books about various dog breeds, this is always the part that I find the most difficult. The problem with having and loving a dog is that, at some point, you are probably going to have to accept the fact that you will outlive your beloved friend.

I promised in the introduction, "About the German Shepherd," that I would take you from puppyhood into the senior years. Having done that, I'm not going to stop just because it would be easier. Let's talk about saying goodbye.

When Should I Let My Dog Go?

You have loved this sweet creature every day of his life, and he's loved you right back. Maybe you've noticed that he's slowing down, and the toys he used to enjoy playing with aren't getting the attention they once did. You're wondering if it's time to let go.

I've loved and lost a few dogs, and at one point, I asked my veterinarian if I should have my friend put to sleep. She said that she couldn't make the decision for me, but that this essay might help me to come to a decision.

A Dog's Prayer

by Beth Norman Harris

Treat me kindly, my beloved master, for no heart in the world is more grateful for kindness than mine. Do not break my spirit with a stick, for although I should lick your hand between the blows, your patience and understanding will teach me more quickly the things that you would have me do.

Speak to me often, for your voice is the world's sweetest music, as you must know by the fierce wagging of my tail when I hear your step. When the weather is cold and wet, please take me inside for I am a domesticated animal, no longer used to bitter elements, and I ask no greater glory than the privilege of sitting at your feet.

Keep my pan filled with fresh water, for although I should not reproach you if it were dry, I cannot tell you when I suffer thirst. Feed me clean food so that I may stay well, to romp and play and do your bidding, to walk by your side standing ready to protect you with my life should your life be in danger.

And master, when I am very old and the Greatest Master sees fit to deprive me of my health and sight, do not turn me away. Rather see that my trusting life is gently taken away and I shall leave you knowing with the last breath I draw, my fate was always safest in your hands.

The end.

So, When Is It Time?

It's when he's not having fun anymore. You have a responsibility to do the right thing. It's hard. It's the hardest decision you'll ever have to make, but your dog has always trusted you to do what's best for him. Don't back away from that responsibility. And if it's humanly possible, be there with your dog when he takes his final breath. Your face should be the last thing he sees.

Once you've said goodbye, don't try to go it alone. Seek help and comfort from family and friends. If you just can't get through it alone, look for pet loss support sites online. And read this:

Rainbow Bridge

Author Unknown

Just this side of heaven is a place called Rainbow Bridge.

When an animal dies that has been especially close to someone here, that pet goes to Rainbow Bridge.

There are meadows and hills for all of our special friends so they can run and play together.

There is plenty of food, water, and sunshine, and our friends are warm and comfortable.

All the animals who had been ill and old are restored to health and vigor; those who were hurt or maimed are made whole and strong again, just as we remember them in our dreams of days and times gone by.

The animals are happy and content, except for one small thing; they each miss someone very special to them, who had to be left behind.

They all run and play together, but the day comes when one suddenly stops and looks into the distance. His bright eyes are intent; His eager body quivers. Suddenly he begins to run from the group, flying over the green grass, his legs carrying him faster and faster.

You have been spotted, and when you and your special friend finally meet, you cling together in joyous reunion, never to be parted again. The happy kisses rain upon your face; your hands again caress the beloved head, and you look once more into the trusting eyes of your pet, so long gone from your life but never absent from your heart.

Then you cross Rainbow Bridge together.

One thing that I have learned, over many years and many dogs, is that the stupidest thing you can do is say, "I'm never going to have another dog." You might not want another dog immediately after losing the one you loved so much, but I think the best way to honor the memory of that dog is to keep the love going. As soon as you're ready, get another dog. You need that kind of love in your life, and there's a dog out there who needs you.

Conclusion

The German Shepherd is a breed with a history of bravery and a stellar work ethic, serving initially as a herding dog, and then later in military and police work. Shepherds have also excelled in search-and-rescue, security, and as guide dogs. Today, the Shepherd is best known as a companion dog and also excels in the show ring.

German Shepherds are usually good with children, and, if properly introduced and supervised, good with other animals. It's very rare that you'll encounter any temperament issues with a German Shepherd, and if you do, you can attribute the responsibility to bad breeders or abusive owners.

German Shepherds don't require much in the way of grooming — a good brushing every so often, perhaps a bath if your Shepherd gets into something really dirty, and you're good to go when it comes to the coat. Ears and paws should be checked regularly for signs of irritation or injury. Regular tooth brushing can prevent dental decay and gum disease. Also, keep your Shepherd's nails trimmed if he's not in the habit of walking on hard surfaces that will naturally wear them down.

Exercise and proper nutrition are essential if you're going to have a happy, healthy, well-adjusted German Shepherd. For adults, this means quality dog food, fed on a schedule or free-fed, and about an hour a day of walking or vigorous play. For puppies, it's quality puppy chow and about five minutes of exercise for each month of the puppy's age. Select toys that are sturdy and will stand up to the treatment a large dog will deliver — don't waste your money at the dollar store.

German Shepherds are typically healthy but there's no such thing as a dog that isn't prone to any disorders whatsoever. Awareness of some of the problems that might (but will not necessarily) occur, combined with regular veterinary checkups, will go a long way to ensure that you have many years to enjoy with your Shepherd.

German Shepherds are easy to train, fairly easy to socialize (although they can be aloof), and very adaptable. If you're contemplating a puppy for your family, and you're comfortable dealing with a large dog that sometimes has a mind of his own, then you'll probably do well with a German Shepherd. There are also adult Shepherds out there that need to be rescued, usually through no fault of their own, so if you have some experience with dogs, and are willing to take an adult dog, I urge you to get in touch with German Shepherd rescue organizations.

Whatever route you choose, be it a puppy or adult German Shepherd, I can virtually guarantee that you will end up with a companion that will please you beyond words, every day of his life. Choose your Shepherd carefully, from a responsible breeder, and make sure to train and socialize.

Sources

https://dogtime.com/dog-breeds/german-shepherd-dog#/

https://images.akc.org/pdf/breeds/standards/GermanShepherdDog.pdf

https://thehappypuppysite.com/german-shepherd-temperament/

https://www.akc.org/dog-breeds/german-shepherd-dog/

https://simplyfordogs.com/puppy-mills/5-reasons-puppy-mills-must-stopped/

https://www.petcarerx.com/article/healthy-eating-for-a-german-shepherd/506#:~:text=German%20shepherd%20dogs%20are%20large,and%202%2C100%20calories%20per%20day.

https://simplyfordogs.com/dogs-food/your-dog-is-not-a-human-so-dont-feed-him-like-one/

https://www.akc.org/expert-advice/health/tips-for-grooming-german-shepherd/

https://www.borrowmydoggy.com/doggypedia/guide-to-dog-breeds/german-shepherd-information-guide#:~:text=How%20much%20exercise%20does%20a,sure%20they%20aren't%20bored.

https://www.thesprucepets.com/steps-to-train-your-dog-1118273

https://www.cesarsway.com/5-essential-commands-you-can-teach-your-dog/

https://en.wikipedia.org/wiki/Harold_Shipman

https://blog.homesalive.ca/adopting-a-rescue-the-first-seven-days

https://thesmartcanine.com/german-shepherds-live-apartment/

http://www.sarbin.com/otis-n-jake/stories/prayer2.html

https://www.petloss.com/rainbowbridge.htm

Printed in Great Britain
by Amazon